KETO
CROCK POT
COOKBOOK
FOR BEGINNERS

THE KETO CROCK POT COOKBOOK FOR BEGINNERS

The Ultimate Ketogenic Low Carb Keto Diet. Delicious, Easy & Healthy Slow Cooker Recipes For Rapid Weight Loss, Healing & A Healthier Lifestyle.

ISBN 978-1-912511-46-4

DISCLAIMER

CONTENTS

SOUPS   77

SUMMER SALADS   87

CONVERSION CHART   95

INTRODUCTION

The combination of high protein, healthy fats and low carb vegetable ingredients mean meal times don't get much heartier and simpler than crock pot Keto meals.

One of the best things about crock pots is that they take care of themselves leaving you to attend to other things. They are also an extremely economical as well as convenient method of cooking. - they don't emit much heat beyond the pot so use far less energy than a conventional oven What better appliance to have in the kitchen to prepare delicious Keto friendly meals?

Our collection of keto crock pot recipes are perfect for those wishing to maintain a balanced, healthy diet based on the Ketogenic principals. All the recipes are calorie counted and where possible make the best of seasonal fresh ingredients.

All of the recipes take no longer than 10-15 minutes to prepare. There are a number of 'shortcut' ingredients like salsa and taco rub throughout the book, but there is also the option to make these from scratch if you have the time. All meat and vegetables should be cut into even sized pieces.

Crock pot Keto meals are particularly good for week-night suppers. Quick to prepare, with no fuss they can be cooked and stored ahead of time ready to warm through for a hearty, perfect meal. The combination of high protein, healthy fats and low carb vegetable ingredients mean meal times don't get much heartier and simpler than crock pot Keto dishes.

Based around the principles of the Keto Diet our crock pot recipes have been uniquely designed to help you manage your weight loss and maintain your goal weight, keeping you inspired and feeling energised each step of the way.

What is the Keto Diet?

Unlike many new modern day diets, the Ketogenic, often shortened to 'Keto' Diet has been in existence for almost 100 years. The diet was originally designed for medical purposes by Dr Russell Wilder in 1924 as an effective method of treating epilepsy. The science upon which the diet was based centres around the process whereby the body enters the state of ketosis as a direct result of the consumption of certain foods in a controlled manner. When higher levels of fats are consumed, together with a reduction in carbohydrates, the liver plays its role in converting these natural fats into fatty acids and ketones. An increased quantity of ketones in the blood system enables ketosis. In this state the body uses fat, not carbohydrates as its primary energy source.

When in ketosis, there are a large number of benefits to the body that can help relieve and ease the symptoms of many other diseases and prevent the onset of many others. What is making the Keto Diet evermore popular is the benefit of weight loss that comes with ketosis.

Some benefits of Ketosis

- Appetite is surpressed: eating more protein and fats makes you feel fuller for longer.
- Weight loss can be quicker: studies show that cutting carbs is a faster method of shedding excess weight.
- Low carbs can be effective in reducing visceral fat in the abdominal area.
- Increased quantities of healthy fats in your diet can raise levels of HDL (High Density Lipoprotein) which is the 'good' cholesterol.
- Carbs are broken down into sugars which then enter the blood stream. This elevates blood sugar levels and as a result the body produces more insulin to combat this. * By cutting carbs you remove the need for increased insulin which if not correctly managed can lead to Type 2 Diabetes.
- A low carb diet can reduce blood pressure leading to a reduced risk of diseases such as stroke, kidney failure and heart disease.

What foods are 'Keto'?

The Keto Diet is high-fat and low-carb, with a reasonable volume of protein. When the Keto Diet refers to fat, it is simply referring to natural fats, not processed or fast-food fats. There are a number of variations to the Keto Diet if using to treat a specific medical condition (for example epilepsy or Parkinson's) however the majority, if not all, rule out sweets, cakes and treats.

The Keto Diet is largely based around meats, mainly red meats and pork, fatty fish, such as tuna and salmon, chicken and turkey, along with a good balance of eggs and dairy, such as butter, cream and unprocessed cheese. This makes the Keto Diet widely accessible, although it is encouraged that, where possible, meats and other animal products are sourced sustainably to ensure the best quality, such as grass-fed, corn-fed and free range.

Healthy oils, nuts, seeds, and healthy herbs, spices and seasonings are equally as important and can be easily added to any meal. In addition, make sure you fill up your plate with low-carb vegetables such as peppers, tomatoes, onions and largely green vegetables. Whilst fruits tend to be eliminated, the avocado is particularly favoured and beneficial in the Keto Diet.

You will find that some of the recipies in this book do include ingredients which may not be strictly keto. This includes sweet potatoes, soy beans, a little fruit and a dash ot two of wine for cooking. However we would term these type of ingredients as ok to include occasionally but are best avoided during the intial introduction process of the diet.

Why eat Keto?

The Keto Diet not only helps enhance and increase the body's metabolic rate to stimulate weight loss, but it also provides several other health benefits and can be used to relieve and treat the symptoms of some illnesses and conditions when planned and managed properly.

When using the Keto Diet for the purpose of weight loss, unlike so many highly restrictive diets, the Keto Diet provides a significant range of foods that you can eat as part of your programme. This enables you to adopt the Keto Diet as a lifestyle change because it is sustainable. Many other diets cannot be followed long-term as they eliminate too many food groups, or would risk causing serious damage to the body, particularly 'fasting' diets.

The Keto Diet is a healthy, controlled and balanced way to help you control and maintain your goal weight and this collection of Keto recipes is specifically designed to help manage weight loss.

How to eat Keto

Eating the 'Keto way' and adhering to a Keto Diet is relatively easy. There are different levels of Keto, as such, depending on how strictly you wish to enforce a weight loss approach. Ratios are often referred to in the Keto Diet (for example 60-75% of calories form healthy fats, 15-30% of calories from protein and 5-10% from carbs) to ensure that your food group portions are appropriately proportioned; for example, whilst bacon and red meats can be eaten, a plate of just steak or a stack of bacon rashers is not going to provide improvements alone. Ensuring that your carbohydrate intake is kept as low as possible in conjunction with increased healthy fats and protein can aid quicker and greater weight loss. Moreover, the flexibility that the Keto Diet offers means that once you are happy with a sustained weight, you can become more liberal with your intake and ratios.

How to lose weight with the Keto Diet

Essentially, the fewer carbohydrates you include with your diet, snacks and meals, the greater weight loss you will see!

The Keto Diet looks to exclude sugary foods, such as cake, chocolate and fruit, as well as alcohol. Whilst at first your body will miss and crave these foods, once the sugar is out of your system and you are past the 'withdrawal' stage, your body will crave foods less. Sugary foods do not keep you full for long and are designed to make your body crave more. By eating healthier alternatives including healthy fats within the Keto Diet, you are likely to feel much fuller for longer, experiencing fewer, if any, cravings and also a generally reduced hunger and appetite. Many Keto Diet followers comment on their reduced appetite noting how they easily go longer between meals and rarely snack at all.

When following the Keto Diet, your body uses fat as its energy supply. With lowered sugar levels come lowered insulin levels, which enables and increases the fat burning process even more so, which is how we see weight loss and weight management as such a substantial side effect of a properly planned and managed Keto Diet programme.

When cooking our Keto one-pot meals you should follow these basic principles to achieve the best results:

Meat

Browning meat is very important. You may be tempted to skip this part but the end results will be inferior if you do. Browning meat gives your dish both flavour and colour and by sealing in hot oil it retains its juices. Don't add too much meat to a saucepan when browning – it's better to brown in batches as a build up of steam in a crowded pan will inhibit the browning process.

Part of the joy of crock pot meals is that tougher cuts of meat can be transformed into delicious and tender bites. The good news for the cook is that cheaper cuts of meat can therefore be used in many recipes.

Trim all meats of any excess fats. While certain cuts of meat such as chicken thighs may be suited to a crock pot recipe, these tend to be much higher in fat and calories so our recipes opt for the leaner cuts of meat wherever possible.

Crock Pot Tips

- All cooking times are a guide.
- Make sure you get to know your own slow cooker so that you can adjust timings accordingly.
- Read the manufacturers operating instructions as appliances can vary. For example, some recommend preheating the slow cooker for 20 minutes before use whilst others advocate switching on only when you are ready to start cooking.
- Slow cookers do not brown-off meat. While not always necessary, if you do prefer to brown your meat you must first do this in a pan with a little low calorie cooking spray.
- A spray of one calorie cooking oil in the cooker before adding ingredients will help with cleaning or you can buy liners.
- Don't be tempted to regularly lift the lid of your appliance while cooking. The seal that is made with the lid on is all part of the slow cooking process. Each time you do lift the lid you will need to increase the cooking time.
- Removing the lid at the end of the cooking time can be useful to thicken up a sauce by adding additional cooking time and continuing to cook without the lid on. On the other hand if perhaps a sauce it too thick removing the lid and adding a little more liquid can help.
- Always add hot liquids to your slow cooker, not cold.
- Do not overfill your slow cooker.
- Allow the inner dish of your slow cooker to completely cool before cleaning. Any stubborn marks can usually be removed after a period of soaking in hot soapy water.
- Be confident with your cooking. Feel free to use substitutes to suit your own taste and don't let a missing herb or spice stop you making a meal - you'll almost always be able to find something to replace it.

About CookNation

CookNation is the leading publisher of innovative and practical recipe books for the modern, health conscious cook.

CookNation titles bring together delicious, easy and practical recipes with their unique non-nonsense approach – making cooking for diet and healthy eating fast, simple and fun.

With a range of #1 best-selling titles – from the innovative 'Skinny' calorie-counted series, to the 5:2 Diet Recipes collection – CookNation recipe books prove that 'Diet' can still mean 'Delicious'!

To browse all CookNation's recipe books visit **www.bellmackenzie.com**

CookNation

CHICKEN DISHES

....

RUSTIC CHICKEN STEW

495 calories per serving

Ingredients

- 2kg/4½ lb skinless chicken pieces
- 2 tbsp almond flour
- 1 onion, chopped
- 1 red (bell) pepper, sliced
- 2 cloves garlic, crushed
- 2 x 400g/14oz cans chopped tomatoes
- 1 tsp dried rosemary

- 1 handful pitted green olives
- 1 tsp anchovy paste
- 3 bay leaves
- 500ml/2 cups chicken stock
- 1 tbsp olive oil
- Salt & pepper to taste

Method

1 Season the chicken pieces well. Dust with the flour and then quickly brown in a large pan with the olive oil.

2 When browned, remove the chicken from the pan and place in the crock pot with all the other ingredients. Leave to cook on low for 5-6 hours or high for 3-4 hours with the lid tightly shut or until the chicken is cooked through and tender.

3 If you prefer the sauce to be a little thicker, continue cooking for about 45 min on the high setting with the lid removed.

CHEFS NOTE

Widely known in Italy as 'Hunter's Stew', this hearty meal has kept the faith with countless hunters and gatherers over the years. Regional variations of this dish are common throughout Italy - this rustic version is one of the most popular.

ASIAN CHICKEN

256
calories per
serving

Ingredients

- 500g/1lb 2oz skinless chicken breasts
- 2 garlic cloves, crushed
- 1 onion, chopped
- 2 tbsp tomato puree/paste
- 4 tbsp light soy sauce

- 200g/7oz green beans
- Pinch crushed chilli
- 250ml/1 cup coconut milk
- 1 tsp sunflower oil

Method

1 Combine all the ingredients in a bowl and add to the crock pot.

2 Cook on low for 5-6 hours or on high for 3-4 hours with the lid tightly shut or until the chicken is cooked through and tender.

3 Add a little water during cooking if needed and serve the chicken shredded with 2 forks.

CHEFS NOTE

Serve with a garnish of scallions/spring onions & sesame seeds.

GREEN PESTO CHICKEN THIGHS

469 calories per serving

Ingredients

- 500g/1lb 2oz skinless, boneless chicken thighs
- 175g/6oz green pesto
- 250ml/1 cup buttermilk
- 1 tsp salt
- 50g/2oz asparagus spears
- 2 cloves garlic, crushed
- 1 onion, chopped

Method

1 Smother the chicken thighs in pesto and carefully combine with all the other ingredients, except the asparagus spears, in the crock pot. Cook on low for 5-6 hours or on high for 3-4 hours with the lid tightly shut.

2 Half an hour before cooking ends add the asparagus spears. Ensure the chicken is cooked through and tender.

3 Serve with fresh green salad and keto friendly bread.

CHEFS NOTE

Originating from Northern Italy, pesto has been around since Ancient Roman times. It's pounded blend of basil, cheese, pine nuts, salt and olive oil create a distinctive taste which works well with meat. Pour any juices from the bottom of the crock pot over the chicken before serving.

SLOW CHICKEN WINGS

433 calories per serving

Ingredients

- 16 large skinless chicken wings
- 1 tsp freshly grated ginger (or ½ tsp ground ginger)
- 2 cloves garlic, crushed
- 1 tbsp light soy sauce
- 1 tsp sesame oil

- 1 tbsp lemon juice
- Handul of radishes, sliced
- 4 scallions/spring onions chopped
- 120ml/½ cup stock
- 2 tsp sesame seeds
- Salt and pepper to taste

Method

1 Combine the chicken wings with all the other ingredients, except the spring onions, radishes and sesame seeds, in the crock pot.

2 Leave to cook on high for approx 4 hours or low for 6 hours.

3 Serve sprinkled with the spring onions, radishes and sesame seeds.

CHEFS NOTE

This is a lovely sweet tender chicken recipe which is great to share with family & friends.

FALL OFF THE BONE WHOLE SLOW COOKED CHICKEN

446 calories per serving

Ingredients

- 2kg/ 4½lb skinless whole chicken broiler
- 2 onions, sliced into rings

- Dried rub mix of :
- 1 tsp each garlic powder, thyme, paprika & onion powder + pinch salt

Method

1 Combine the dried ingredients together and rub really well into the fresh chicken.

2 Place the onions in the bottom of the crock pot and put the chicken on top. Cook on low for 7-8 hours with the lid tightly shut. Ensure the chicken is cooked through.

3 Serve with your choice of non starchy keto vegetables or salad.

CHEFS NOTE

Whole cooked chicken really comes into it's own in the crock pot. This super simple recipe will give you the heart of a meal which, with leftovers, can last a couple of days.

ZINGY LIME CHICKEN

200 calories per serving

Ingredients

- 500g/1lb 2oz skinless chicken breasts
- 3 tbsp lime juice
- Bunch fresh cilantro/coriander chopped and some to garnish
- 1 sliced green chilli (or a pinch of dried chilli flakes)
- 400g/14oz salsa (or make your own)
- 4 tsp taco seasoning (or make your own)

Salsa: Add 1 onion chopped, 1 clove garlic crushed, 1 green chilli chopped to 2 x 400g/14oz cans chopped tomatoes + sea salt to taste

Taco Seasoning: 2 tsp mild chilli powder, 1 ½ tsp ground cumin, ½ tsp paprika, ¼ tsp each of onion powder, garlic powder, dried oregano & crushed chilli flakes, 1 tsp each of sea salt & black pepper

Method

1 Put everything together in the crock pot making sure the chicken is covered with the rest of the ingredients. With the lid tightly shut, leave to cook for 4-5 hours on high or 5-6 hours on the low setting.

2 Ensure the chicken is cooked through and tender then shred it a little with 2 forks and serve with a fresh green salad and almond flour wraps.

CHEFS NOTE

Packed with protein, skinless chicken breasts are a great low fat meat to use in the crock pot. The citrus lightness of this recipe is perfect. for summer months as well as a welcome taste bud infusion during the colder seasons.

FRESH BASIL & PARMESAN CHICKEN STEW

380 calories per serving

Ingredients

- 2 onions, sliced
- 2 garlic cloves, crushed
- 500g/1lb 2oz skinless chicken breasts, cubed
- 60ml/¼ cup chicken broth/stock
- 200g/7oz baby courgettes, sliced lengthways
- 400g/14oz fresh ripe plum tomatoes
- 50g/2oz Parmesan cheese
- 1 large bunch fresh basil, roughly chopped
- 2 tsp olive oil
- Salt & pepper to taste

Method

1 Gently sauté the onion & garlic in the olive oil for a few minutes until softened.

2 Place in the crock pot with all the other ingredients, except the Parmesan cheese. (Reserve a little fresh basil for garnish).

3 Cover and leave to cook on low for 3-4 hours or until the chicken is cooked through. Season and serve.

CHEFS NOTE

Feel free to use canned tomatoes if you don't have fresh tomatoes to hand.

CHICKEN & ALMONDS

320 calories per serving

Ingredients

- 500g/1lb 2oz skinless chicken breasts, cut into chunks
- 1 tbsp ground almonds
- ½ tsp paprika
- 2 red (bell) peppers, sliced
- 1 onion, chopped
- 2 cloves garlic, crushed
- 1 tbsp white wine vinegar
- 2 tbsp chopped flat leaf parsley
- 400g/14oz can chopped tomatoes
- ½ tsp dried chilli flakes
- 100g/3½oz spinach
- 2 tsp olive oil
- Salt & pepper to taste

Method

1 Brown the chicken pieces in the olive oil.

2 Add all the ingredients, except the parsley, into the crock pot. Season, cover and leave to cook on high for 3-4 hours or low for 5-6 hours.

3 Sprinkle with chopped parsley and serve.

CHEFS NOTE

This Spanish inspired dish is great as a main meal but can also be served as a delicious keto friendly pizza topping.

BBQ CHICKEN

230
calories per
serving

Ingredients

- 450g/1lb skinless chicken breasts
- 1 tsp each, smoked paprika & garlic powder
- 60ml/¼ cup chicken broth/stock
- ½ tsp each ground cumin & ground cilantro/coriander

- 2 tsp stevia
- 3 tbsp Worcestershire sauce
- ½ tsp salt
- 3 tbsp tomato puree/paste or ketchup

Method

1 Put all the ingredients into the crock pot. Mix well, cover and leave to cook on low for 4-5 hours or until the chicken is cooked through and tender.

2 Shred the chicken breasts with 2 forks and mix back into the sauce at the bottom of the crock pot.

3 If the sauce needs to be thickened, continue to cook on high for up to 45 mins with the lid off. Alternatively if it's too sticky, add a little water to loosen up.

4 Serve with salad and BBQ sauce.

CHEFS NOTE

When the chicken is shredded and mixed back into the sauce, you should be left with a moist versatile mixture which is effectively the poultry version of the BBQ classic 'pulled pork'.

LOVELY LEMONY GARLICKY CHICKEN

208 calories per serving

Ingredients

- 500g/1lb 2oz skinless chicken breasts
- 3 garlic cloves, crushed
- 3 tbsp lemon juice
- 1 onion, chopped
- 1 tsp stevia

- 1 tsp almond flour dissolved in a little water to make a paste
- 500ml/2 cups chicken broth/stock
- Salt & pepper to taste
- Bunch fresh basil, chopped

Method

1 Combine all the ingredients in the crock pot and leave to cook on low for 5-6 hours or on high for 3-4 hours with the lid tightly shut. Ensure the chicken is cooked through and tender.

2 Serve with steamed vegetables and cauliflower 'rice' to soak up the juices.

CHEFS NOTE

This is a really simple protein-packed dish that really benefits from using fresh basil.

LUSCIOUS ITALIAN CHICKEN

SERVES 4

285 calories per serving

Ingredients

- 500g/1lb 2oz skinless chicken breasts
- 2 x 400g/14oz cans condensed chicken or mushroom soup
- 100g/3½ oz mushrooms, sliced
- 1 onion, chopped
- Salt & pepper to taste

- 1 garlic clove, crushed
- 2 tbsp cream cheese

Dried rub mix of:
- 1 teaspoon each oregano, rosemary & thyme

Method

1 Rub the chicken breasts with the dried herb mix and combine all the ingredients into the crock pot. Cook on low for 5-6 hours or on high for 3-4 hours with the lid tightly shut.

2 Ensure the chicken is cooked through and tender; try serving with shredded courgette 'noodles'.

CHEFS NOTE
With a lovely creamy consistency, this Italian inspired dish makes the most of that wonderful 'cheat' ingredient - condensed soup!

PEANUT BUTTER CHICKEN

245
calories per serving

Ingredients

- 500g/1lb 2oz skinless chicken breast, diced
- 1 red (bell) pepper, sliced
- 1 onion, chopped
- 4 tbsp low fat peanut butter
- 2 tbsp lime juice
- 120ml/½ cup chicken broth/stock

- 1 tbsp soy sauce
- 1 tsp each ground cumin & cilantro/coriander
- ½ tsp paprika
- Salt & pepper to taste
- 2 tsp olive oil

Method

1 In a frying pan quickly brown the chicken in the olive oil.

2 Add all the ingredients to the crock pot, season, cover and leave to cook on low for 4-5 hours or high for 3-4 hours.

3 Make sure the chicken is cooked through and serve with stir fry veggies & beansprouts.

CHEFS NOTE

Peanut butter chicken is delicious. You can really 'lift' the dish by serving with fresh lime wedges.

MUSTARD TARRAGON CHICKEN

352 calories per serving

Ingredients

- 500g/1lb 2oz skinless chicken breasts
- 2 tbsp fresh chopped tarragon
- 1 tsp mild mustard, or more to taste
- 400g/14oz canned black soy beans
- 500ml/2 cups chicken broth/stock
- 300g/11oz tenderstem broccoli
- 2 tsp olive oil
- Salt & pepper to taste
- 3 tbsp crème fraiche or Greek yogurt

Method

1 Quickly brown the chicken breast in the oil for a few mins.

2 Place all the ingredients, except the crème fraiche, in the crock pot and season well. Cover and leave to cook on high for 2-3 hours or until the chicken is tender and cooked through.

3 Remove the chicken from the crock pot, stir through the crème fraiche and pour the beans, veg & sauce over the chicken.

CHEFS NOTE

Unlike most beans black soy beans are a great low carb keto ingredient.

SIMPLE CHICKEN CURRY

323 calories per serving

Ingredients

- 500g/1lb 2oz skinless chicken breasts
- 1 onion, chopped
- 1 tbsp tomato puree/paste
- 3 cloves garlic, crushed
- 1 tsp butter
- 1 tbsp fresh grated ginger (or use 1 tsp of ginger powder)
- 1 tsp garam masala
- 1 tsp ground cumin
- 1 tsp turmeric
- ½ tsp chilli powder
- 4 tbsp coconut cream
- 375ml/1 ½ cups tomato sauce/passata
- Salt & pepper to taste

Method

1 Combine all the ingredients, except the coconut cream into the crock pot. Cook on low for 5-6 hours or on high for 3-4 hours with the lid tightly shut.

2 Ensure the chicken is cooked through and tender, stir in the coconut cream to warm through for a few minutes.

3 Try serving with green beans and keto friendly flat bread.

CHEFS NOTE
The mix of spices suggested in the recipe is preferable but it is fine to substitute with curry powder if you are in a rush or struggling with store cupboard ingredients.

SERVES 4

CHIPOTLE CHICKEN

198
calories per
serving

Ingredients

- 500g/1lb 2oz skinless chicken breasts
- 1 onion, finely chopped
- 1 red onion, sliced
- 3 garlic cloves, crushed
- 2 tsp chipotle paste
- 1 400g/14oz can chopped tomatoes
- 2 tbsp fresh chopped flat leaf parsley
- 2 tsp sunflower oil
- Salt & pepper to taste

Method

1 Gently sauté the onion and garlic in the sunflower oil. Remove and quickly brown the chicken breasts in the same pan.

2 Add all the ingredients, except the red onion and parsley, into the crock pot. Season, cover and leave to cook on high for 2-3 hours or low for 4-5 hours until the meat is tender and cooked through.

3 Shred the chicken with two forks, mix well and serve with the parsley and raw red onion slices on top. Also good with a dollop of Greek yogurt on the side.

CHEFS NOTE

Chipotle paste is essentially smokey chilli paste from the Mexican Chipotle chilli. If you have difficulty sourcing, just substitute for regular chillies and a little smoked paprika.

CHICKEN & MUSTARD LEEKS

290 calories per serving

Ingredients

- 500g/1lb 2oz skinless chicken breasts
- 1 tbsp almond flour
- 100g/3½oz back bacon
- 2 leeks, chopped
- 2 tbsp Dijon mustard
- 1 tsp mustard powder
- 250ml/1 cup chicken broth/stock
- 200g/7oz butternut squash, cubed
- 1 bay leaf
- 300g/11oz spinach
- 1 tbsp olive oil
- Salt & pepper to taste

Method

1 Season the chicken and coat well in the flour. Add the olive oil to a frying pan and quickly brown the breasts.

2 Add all the ingredients to the crock pot, cover, stir well and leave to cook on high for 2-3 hours or low for 4-5 hours.

3 Remove the chicken & veg from the crock pot and ladle over as much of the sauce as you prefer. .

CHEFS NOTE

The mustard in this recipe should be adjusted to your own taste. You can also use wholegrain mustard if you prefer.

CHICKEN & GARLIC

289 calories per serving

Ingredients

- 500g/1lb 2oz skinless chicken breasts
- 1 lemon, sliced
- 2 onions, chopped
- 6 garlic cloves, sliced
- 250ml/1 cup chicken broth/stock
- 150g/5oz green beans
- 2 tsp olive oil
- Salt & pepper to taste

Method

1 Season the chicken. Add the oil to a frying pan and quickly brown the breasts.

2 Add all the ingredients to the crock pot. Cover, stir well and leave to cook on high for 2-3 hours or low for 4-5 hours.

3 Serve with keto friendly crusty bread to mop up the delicious lemon juices. If you need more liquid during cooking add a little more stock.

CHEFS NOTE
If you prefer your beans crunchy you can hold off adding them until about 20 minutes before the end of cooking.

CHICKEN & APRICOTS

225
calories per serving

Ingredients

- 500g/1lb 2oz skinless chicken breasts
- 1 tbsp almond flour
- 2 garlic cloves, crushed
- 1 tbsp freshly grated ginger
- 1 tsp each ground cumin & cilantro/coriander
- ½ tsp ground cinnamon
- 1 tbsp lemon juice
- 4 fresh apricots
- ½ cup/120ml chicken broth/stock
- Salt & pepper to taste

Method

1 Mix the flour, cinnamon, cumin & coriander together and combine with the chicken breasts.

2 Add all the other ingredients, to the crock pot. Stir well, cover and leave to cook on high for 2-3 hours or low for 4-5 hours (adding more stock during cooking if needed).

3 Serve with steamed greens.

CHEFS NOTE
Apricots are fine to use as an 'occasional' ingredient in keto cooking.

KETO
CROCK POT
COOKBOOK
FOR BEGINNERS

BEEF DISHES

....

ITALIAN MEATBALLS

323 calories per serving

Ingredients

- 650g/1lb 7oz lean, minced/ground beef
- 1 slice keto friendly bread, whizzed into breadcrumbs
- ½ onion, finely chopped
- Handful fresh parsley, chopped
- 1 large free range egg

- 1 clove garlic, crushed
- ½ tsp salt
- 2 400g/14 oz cans chopped tomatoes
- 2 tbsp tomato puree/paste
- 250ml/1 cup beef broth/stock
- 1 tsp each dried basil, oregano & thyme

Method

1 Combine together the beef, breadcrumbs, egg, onion, garlic and half the salt. (You can do it with your hands or for super-speed put it all into a food mixer).

2 Once the ingredients are properly mixed together, use your hands to shape into about 20-24 meat balls. Add all the ingredients to the crock pot and combine well.

3 Cover and leave to cook on low for 5-6 hours or 3-4 hours on high. Ensure the beef is well cooked and serve with parmesan and a green salad.

CHEFS NOTE

Meatballs are easy to make and never a disappointment to eat. The simple sauce accompanying the meat here is lovely as it is, but a dash of Worcestershire sauce or a tsp of marmite will give it additional depth.

BUDAPEST'S BEST BEEF GOULASH

228
calories per serving

Ingredients

- 900g/2lbs lean stewing beef cut into chunks (trim off any fat)
- 1 red (bell) pepper, sliced
- 3 cloves garlic, crushed
- 250ml/1 cup beef broth/stock or water
- 400g/14oz can chopped tomatoes
- 1 tbsp tomato puree/paste
- 1 tsp paprika
- 1½ tbsp almond flour
- 1 onion, chopped
- 2 tsp olive oil
- Salt & pepper to taste

Method

1 Season the beef and quickly brown in a smoking hot pan with the olove oil.

2 Remove from the pan and dust with flour (the easiest way is to put the beef and flour into a plastic bag and give it a good shake).

3 Add all the ingredients to the crock pot and combine well. Leave to cook on low with the lid tightly shut for 5-6 hours or until the beef is tender and cooked through (add a little more stock during cooking if needed).

4 Lovely served with a salad & sour cream.

CHEFS NOTE
Goulash is a European dish which suits the crock pot beautifully. After hours of gentle cooking this 'tougher' meat becomes a tender cut which just melts in the mouth.

GINGER BEEF & EGG PLANT/AUBERGINES

338 calories per serving

Ingredients

- 675g/1½lb silverside beef/round steak, cubed
- 2 garlic cloves, crushed
- 370ml/1½ cups beef broth/stock
- 1 red (bell) pepper, sliced
- 2 egg plant/aubergine, cubed
- 1 onion, chopped

- 2 tbsp soy sauce
- 1 tbsp freshly grated ginger
- 1 tbsp almond flour mixed with 3 tbsp water to form a paste
- 100g/3½oz green beans
- Salt & pepper to taste

Method

1 Add all the ingredients, except the green beans, to the crock pot.

2 Season well, cover and leave to cook on low for 5-6 hours or high for 3-4 hours.

3 An hour before the end of cooking, add the green beans and continue to cook until both the beef and green beans are tender.

CHEFS NOTE

Ginger and beef are a great combination and often used in Chinese cookery. Use low salt soy sauce if you want to be extra healthy.

CHILLI CON CARNE

SERVES 4

440
calories per serving

Ingredients

- 550g/1¼ lb lean, minced/ground beef
- 400g/14oz can chopped tomatoes
- 1 large onion, chopped
- 250ml/1 cup beef broth/stock
- 250ml/1 cup tomato sauce/passata

- 1 tsp each of oregano, cumin, chilli powder, paprika & garlic powder
- ½ tsp salt
- 2 tsp olive oil

Method

1 Brown the mince and onions in a frying pan with the oil.

2 Add all the ingredients into the crock pot and combine well. Leave to cook on low for 5-6 hours or high for 3-4 hours with the lid tightly closed.

3 Once the meat is fully cooked through, serve with steamed greens and a dollop of crème fraiche.

CHEFS NOTE

The Spanish name simply means 'chilli with meat' and this dish has been a Tex-Mex classic since before the days of the American frontier settlers. Slow cooking the mince beef really allows the flavour to develop.

ENCHILADA EL SALVADOR

324
calories per serving

Ingredients

- 450g/1lb lean, minced/ground beef
- 1 onion, chopped
- 1 green (bell) pepper, chopped
- 1 400g/14oz black soy beans, drained
- 2 400g/14oz cans chopped tomatoes
- 250ml/1 cup beef broth/stock or boiling water
- ½ tsp chilli powder

- 4 tsp taco seasoning

Or make your own seasoning:
- 2 tsp mild chilli powder, 1 ½ tsp ground cumin, ½ tsp paprika, ¼ tsp each of onion powder, garlic powder, dried oregano & crushed chilli flakes, 1 tsp each of sea salt & black pepper

Method

1 Add all the ingredients to the crock pot and combine well.

2 Leave to cook on low with the lid tightly on for 5-6 hours or 3-4 hours on high, until the beef is tender and cooked through. If you want to thicken it up a little leave, to cook for a further 45 mins with the lid off.

3 Serve with keto friendly flour tortillas, shredded salad, grated cheese and sour cream.

CHEFS NOTE
Black soy beans are a useful low carb keto ingredient which differ from the high carb content of most other beans.

BEST BEEF BRISKET

300
calories per
serving

Ingredients

- 2¼ kg/5 lbs beef brisket trimmed of fat
- 4 large onions, sliced into rounds
- 500ml/2 cups beef broth/stock
- 4 bay leaves
- 3 garlic cloves, peeled
- Salt & pepper to taste

Method

1 Season the brisket generously with salt and pepper and brown quickly in a smoking hot dry pan.

2 Lay the onion slices on the bottom of the crock pot and add the beef along with the rest of the ingredients.

3 Leave to cook with the lid tightly on for 7-9 hours on low. It's best to turn over half way through cooking but don't worry too much if you can't do that. Ensure the beef is super-tender and cooked through. Leave to rest for 20 minutes before slicing.

CHEFS NOTE

Brisket is another beef cut which really benefits from the crock pot as it tenderizes slowly and evenly in its own juices without drying it out.

SLOW SCOTTISH 'STOVIES'

333
calories per
serving

Ingredients

- 175g/6oz pumpkin, diced
- 2 large onions, chopped
- 250ml/1 cup vegetable broth/stock
- 450g/1lb left over roast beef (or other cooked red meat)
- Salt & pepper to taste

Method

1 Combine all the ingredients together in the crock pot and cook on low for 5-6 hours or high for 3-4 hours with the lid tightly shut.

2 The liquid should all be gone by the end of the cooking time, if it hasn't, remove the lid and leave to cook for a little longer.

3 Stir through and serve in bowls with British brown sauce if you have it!

CHEFS NOTE
This is a great recipe to use up any cooked leftover red meat you might have. Traditionally it's served with plain Scottish oatcakes and it's super-simple to make. You can also used cubed corned beef in this recipe.

RAGU A LA BOLOGNESE

344 calories per serving

Ingredients

- 500g/1lb 2oz lean, minced/ground beef
- 400g/14oz can chopped tomatoes
- 250ml/1 cup tomato sauce/passata
- 1 tsp each dried oregano & thyme
- 1 stick celery chopped
- 2 bay leaves
- 1 tbsp tomato puree/paste
- 3 garlic cloves, crushed
- 2 onions, chopped
- Salt and pepper to taste
- 2 tsp olive oil

Method

1 Quickly brown the meat in a frying pan with the olive oil. Combine all the ingredients in the crock pot and close the lid tightly.

2 Leave to cook on low for 5-6 hours or high for 3-4 hours.

3 Make sure the meat is cooked through and serve with spiralized veggie spaghetti.

CHEFS NOTE

Nothing can be simpler or more satisfying than bolognese. You can add mushrooms and peppers to the recipe if you like, plus a dash or two of Worcestershire sauce gives extra depth.

PEPPERS & STEAK

250
calories per
serving

Ingredients

- 450g/1lb braising steak/beef chuck
- 120ml/½ cup soy sauce
- 2 tsp ground black pepper
- 3 cloves garlic, crushed

- 3 red or green (bell) peppers, sliced
- 2 onions, chopped
- 120ml/½ cup beef broth/stock

Method

1 Slice the steak and vegetables then add everything to the crock pot,

2 Season, cover and leave to cook on low for 3-5 hours or until the meat is tender and cooked through. (Add a little extra stock during cooking if needed). .

CHEFS NOTE
By slow cooking for a few hours the braising steak should be transformed into a tender cut which can be served as the heart of a lovely warm salad.

ALMONDS, BEEF & OLIVES

392 calories per serving

Ingredients

- 600g/1lb 5oz lean stewing steak/chuck steak, cubed
- 250ml/1 cup beef broth/stock
- 1 tsp each smoked paprika, dried basil & rosemary
- 1 tbsp almond flour
- 200g/7oz pitted olives
- 25g/1oz chopped almonds
- Salt & pepper to taste

Method

1 Season the beef and coat well in the flour.

2 Add all the ingredients, except the olives, to the crock pot and leave to cook on low for 4-6 hours or until the beef is tender.

3 Add a little more stock or wine during cooking if needed and adjust the seasoning. 20 minutes before the end of cooking add the olives, warm through and serve.

CHEFS NOTE

This dish is delicious served with creamed spinach. Feel free to use a different mix of dried herbs to suit your taste. You can also add a tablespoon of tomato puree during cooking to thicken if you prefer.

PORTABELLA MUSHROOMS & CHILLI STEAK CASSEROLE

300 calories per serving

Ingredients

- 2 red peppers, thinly sliced
- 2 onions, sliced
- 2 garlic cloves, finely sliced
- 4 large portabella mushrooms
- 500g/1lb 2oz lean beef stewing steak
- 2 tbsp soy sauce

- 2 tbsp Worcestershire sauce
- 60ml/¼ cup beef broth/stock
- 1 bunch scallions/spring onions, sliced lengthways into ribbons
- 2 tsp olive oil
- Salt & pepper to taste

Method

1 Gently sauté the peppers, onions, garlic & mushrooms in the olive oil until softened.

2 Add the sautéed vegetables to the crock pot along with all the other ingredients, except the spring onions.

3 Gently combine, cover and leave to cook on low for 7-9 hours or until the beef is meltingly tender (add a little more stock during cooking if needed).

4 Season and serve with the sliced spring onions on top.

CHEFS NOTE
Large flat Portabella mushrooms are available all year round but they are at their best in the spring.

KETO
CROCK POT
COOKBOOK
FOR BEGINNERS

PORK DISHES

....

PERFECT PULLED PORK

280 calories per serving

Ingredients

- 900g/2lb pork butt (shoulder)
- 1 onion, chopped
- 250ml/1 cup sugar free BBQ sauce or ketchup
- 250ml/1 cup beef broth/stock or boiling water

- 1 packet BBQ dry rub

Or make your own:
- 1 tbsp each of garlic powder & onion powder,
- celery salt, paprika + 1 tsp each mild chilli powder & cumin

Method

1 Combine all the spices together and cover the pork in the dry spice rub. Add the stock, onion & BBQ sauce and then place the pork on top. Leave to cook on high for 6-8 hours with the lid tightly closed. Ideally you should turn the pork over half way through cooking, but if you can't do that don't worry.

2 Once the pork is tender remove it from the crock pot. Leave to rest for as long as you can resist and then use your hands or 2 forks to pull the pork apart.

3 Once it's all shredded, place in a bowl and remove the cooking liquid from the crock pot. Pour the liquid onto the pork to make beautiful juicy meat.

CHEFS NOTE

Pulled pork is an absolute classic. It's a chance to use almost everything in your spice rack to create a 'killer' dry rub and it always packs an irresistible punchy and more-ish taste.

SAUSAGES & SPINACH

309 calories per serving

Ingredients

- 12 lean, pork or beef sausages (skins removed)
- 2 tsp olive oil
- 250ml/1 cup tomato sauce/passata
- 1 tsp dried rosemary
- 1 splash red wine vinegar
- ½ tsp salt
- 400g/14oz can chopped tomatoes
- 2 tbsp tomato puree
- 2 red peppers, sliced
- 150g/5oz fresh spinach, chopped

Method

1 Brown the sausage meat in a frying pan with the olive oil and break up well.

2 Add all the ingredients, except the spinach, to the crock pot and combine. Close the lid tightly and leave to cook on high for 3-4 hours.

3 When the meat is well cooked, stir in the fresh spinach and leave to cook for a further 10 mins.

CHEFS NOTE

This lovely recipe uses sausage meat to create a thick, luxurious sauce. Use whole meat sausages which are free of fillers such a breadcrumbs.

COWBOY CASSEROLE

414
calories per serving

Ingredients

- 16 lean pork sausages
- 2 400g/14oz cans chopped tomatoes
- 1 onion, chopped
- 4 yellow peppers, sliced
- 1 tbsp tomato puree/paste
- 2 tsp Dijon/mild mustard
- 2 tsp olive oil
- 2 tsp paprika
- 2 tbsp sour cream

Method

1 Brown the sausages in the pan with the onions and olive oil.

2 Combine all the ingredients (except the sour cream) in the crock pot and leave to cook for 3-4 hours on high or low for 5-6 hours with the lid tightly shut.

3 Check the sausages are properly cooked through and, if you want to thicken the sauce up, leave the lid off while you cook on high for up to 45 mins extra.

4 Dollop the sour cream on top and serve with steamed green veg.

CHEFS NOTE
Sausages work on a keto diet when they are free of fillers such a breadcrumbs.

AROMATIC KICKING PORK RIBS

448 calories per serving

Ingredients

- 1kg/2¼ lbs pork ribs
- 1 tsp each garlic powder, chilli, cumin & basil
- ½ tsp salt
- 2 400g/14oz cans chopped tomatoes
- 1 tbsp tomato puree/paste
- 1 green chilli, chopped or a pinch of crushed chilli flakes to taste

Method

1 Rub the dry spices onto the ribs.

2 Add all the ingredients to the crock pot and leave to cook with the lid tightly on for 5-6 hours on low.

3 Ensure the ribs are super tender and serve with rice and beans.

CHEFS NOTE
There are a number of different types of rib available depending on the cut from which they are taken. Choose whichever is cheapest or whichever you prefer. All will work well with this recipe.

CUMIN PORK

366
calories per serving

Ingredients

- 400g/14oz can black soy beans, drained
- 300g/11oz lean boneless pork shoulder, cubed
- 1 onion, chopped
- 4 garlic cloves, crushed
- 1 tsp sunflower oil
- 1 tsp ground cumin
- ½ tsp turmeric
- 250ml/1 cup vegetable broth/stock
- Salt & pepper to taste

Method

1 Quickly brown the cubed pork in a frying pan with the sunflower oil.

2 Add all the ingredients to the crock pot and season well. Cover and leave to cook on high for 3-4 hours or low for 5-6 hours, or until the pork is tender and cooked through.

3 If you want to thicken the sauce a little, leave the lid off and cook for an additional 45 mins, or until you have the consistency you prefer.

CHEFS NOTE

Black soy beans are a useful low carb keto ingredient which differ from the high carb content of most other beans.

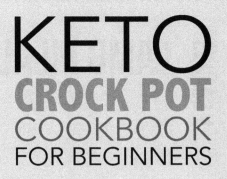

LAMB DISHES

....

LAMB PILAU PAZAR

360 calories per serving

Ingredients

- 500g/1lb 2oz lean lamb cut into bite sized chunks (any lean cut will work for this recipe)
- 1 large onion, chopped
- 200g/7oz tenderstem broccoli
- 1 stick celery, chopped
- 400g/14oz can chopped tomatoes
- 1 tsp dried crushed chilli flakes
- 300g/11oz cauliflower 'rice'
- 500ml/2 cups vegetable broth/stock
- 1 cinnamon stick or ½ tsp ground cinnamon
- Salt & pepper to taste
- 2 tsp olive oil

Method

1 Gently sauté the onion in the olive oil. Remove from the pan and then brown off the lamb for a couple of minutes on a high heat.

2 Combine all the ingredients together in the crock pot, except the 'rice'. Cover and cook on low for 4-6 hours, add the 'rice' and cook for 30 mins or everything is tender and cooked through.

3 If any additional liquid remains, cook on a high heat with the lid off for a further 45 minutes or until the liquid is absorbed into the rice.

4 If you want to add garnish serve with toasted pine nuts, chopped cilantro/coriander or crushed almonds.

CHEFS NOTE

This is a no rice 'pilau' which makes use of cauliflower 'rice which is a great low carb alternative for the keto diet.

SPINACH & LAMB STEW

460
calories per serving

Ingredients

- 500g/1lb 2oz lean lamb cut into bite sized chunks (any lean cut will work)
- 2 cloves garlic, crushed
- Zest of 1 lemon
- 1 onion, chopped
- 2 400g/14oz cans chopped tomatoes
- 1 tbsp tomato puree/paste
- 400g/14oz pumpkin, cubed

- 400g/14oz fresh spinach, chopped
- Dried herb mix of the following:
- 1 tsp each cilantro/coriander & turmeric
- ½ tsp each ground cumin, black pepper & oregano
- 2 tbsp Greek yogurt
- Salt & pepper to taste
- 2 tsp olive oil

Method

1 Gently sauté the onion in the olive oil.

2 Remove from the pan and then brown the lamb for a couple of minutes on a high heat.

3 Combine all ingredients together (except the yogurt and spinach) in the crock pot with the lid tightly shut and cook on low for 4-6 hours or until the lamb is tender and cooked through.

4 30mins before the end of cooking add the spinach, stir through the yogurt before serving.

CHEFS NOTE

Super rich in iron & calcium, spinach is a super-food which is twinned beautifully in this dish with lemon zest and Greek inspired spices.

MARRAKESH LAMB

415
calories per serving

Ingredients

- 500g/1lb 2oz trimmed lamb cut into cubes (any lean cut will work)
- ½ tsp black pepper
- 1 tsp each ground cumin, coriander, ginger, turmeric & paprika
- 1 tsp cinnamon

- 2 400g/14oz cans chopped tomatoes
- 200g/7oz black soy beans
- 250ml/1 cup lamb broth/stock
- 2 onions, chopped
- 5 cloves garlic, crushed

Method

1 This one couldn't be any easier. No need to brown the meat, so just combine all the ingredients in the crock pot, cover and leave to cook on low for 4-6 hours.

2 Ensure the lamb is tender and cooked through. If you want to thicken up a little, leave to cook for a further 45 mins with the lid off.

3 Delicious served with Greek yogurt and fresh Greek herbs.

CHEFS NOTE

Morocco's capital is world renowned for its tagine cuisine. Crock pots provide a wonderful alternative to this specialist style of cooking. This recipe is a lovely North African inspired dish which, if its new to you, should piqué your interest in Moroccan cooking.

LAMB & SAAG SPINACH

320 calories per serving

Ingredients

- 500g/1lb 2oz lean lamb shoulder, cubed
- 1 tsp each fenugreek & mustard seeds
- 1 tsp each ground cumin & ginger
- 2 cloves garlic, crushed
- 250ml/1 cup beef broth/stock
- 400g/14oz spinach
- 4 tbsp Greek yogurt
- 1 tsp mint sauce (shop bought)

Method

1 Other than the yogurt and mint sauce add all the ingredients to the crock pot, cover and leave to cook on low for 4-6 hours or until the lamb is tender.

2 Stir the yogurt and mint sauce through and serve straight away.

CHEFS NOTE

Saag means 'leaf' dish in Indian cuisine. You could try out other green leaves as an alternative to spinach if you prefer.

SEAFOOD DISHES

GREEN THAI FISH CURRY

380 calories per serving

······· *Ingredients* ·······

- 500g/1lb 2oz meaty white fish fillets (go for whatever is on sale) cod, pollack or tilapia
- 3 onions, chopped
- 1 tsp fresh ginger or ½ tsp ground ginger
- 3 cloves garlic, crushed
- 150g/5oz green beans
- 1 red chilli, chopped
- 50g/2oz watercress
- 2 tbsp Thai green curry paste
- 500ml/2 cups coconut milk
- 2 tsp olive oil
- Salt & pepper to taste

······· *Method* ·······

1 Sauté the onions & green beans with the ginger and garlic over a low heat in the olive oil.

2 Season the fish fillets and combine all the ingredients (except the watercress) in the crock pot. Cook on low for 1 ½ hours with the lid tightly shut.

3 Check the fish is properly cooked through by flaking it a little with a fork and gently add the watercress salad to the mix before serving.

4 If you want to make it a little spicier you could add some more chopped chilli or crushed chilli flakes.

CHEFS NOTE
Compared to meat, fish cooks more quickly in the crock pot and as such fish recipes can be really handy if you haven't got too much cooking time. This recipe is a fantastic and easy Thai curry which is simple to prepare and doesn't take long at all in the crock pot.

SWEET & CITRUS SALMON

270 calories per serving

Ingredients

- 500g/1lb 2oz thick boneless salmon fillets
- 1 onion, chopped
- 1 tbsp soy sauce
- 3 tbsp Lime juice
- 2 garlic cloves, crushed
- 1 tbsp sugar free ketcup brushed onto the fillets
- 2 tsp olive oil
- Salt & pepper to taste

Method

1 Chop the onion and sauté for a couple of minutes with the garlic in the olive oil.

2 Remove from the pan and carefully combine all the ingredients in the crock pot. Cook on low for 1½ hours with the lid tightly on.

3 Check the fish is properly cooked by flaking it a little with a fork and serve with a lovely warm salad served and a little crusty keto friendly bread.

CHEFS NOTE

Salmon can be relatively expensive so you can substitute for tilapia or basa or talk to your fishmonger for recommendations.

TUNA & NOODLE CATTIA

260 calories per serving

Ingredients

- 350g/12oz 'miracle' noodles
- 1 onion, chopped
- 400g/14oz can fat free condensed mushroom soup
- 400g/14oz canned tuna steaks or flakes in water
- 100g/3½ oz green beans, chopped
- 1 tsp garlic powder
- Salt & pepper to taste
- Pinch of crushed chilli flakes

Method

1 Quickly cook the noodles in salted boiling water.

2 Save 3 tbsp of the drained water and then combine all the ingredients and saved water in the crock pot. Cover and leave to cook on low for 1½ hours.

3 This is great served with a sliced red onion & tomato salad and a little parmesan.

CHEFS NOTE

An absolute classic crock pot recipe, Tuna & Noodle casserole is always a winner. This version keto version uses 'miracle' noodles which are widley availible and contain zero carbs

CORIANDER & GARLIC SHRIMPS

370 calories per serving

Ingredients

- 500g/1lb 2oz raw jumbo shrimps/king prawns
- 200g/7oz green beans
- 1 tsp sunflower oil
- 2 onions, sliced
- 200g/8oz cherry tomatoes, halved
- 1 tsp ground ginger
- 4 garlic cloves, crushed
- 3 tbsp curry paste
- 2 tbsp fresh chopped coriander/cilantro + extra for garnish
- 250ml/1 cup tomato sauce/passata
- Salt & pepper to taste

Method

1 Add all the ingredients to the crock pot, cover and leave to cook on low for 1-2 hours or until the shrimps are cooked through and the beans are tender.

2 Sprinkle with chopped coriander and serve with rice.

CHEFS NOTE

This is a really simple 'cheat' curry using curry paste. If you want a slightly different taste you could use less passata and add a little coconut milk to the recipe after cooking.

245

calories per serving

SERVES 4

FISH STEW

Ingredients

- 450g/1lb white fish fillets, cubed
- 1 leek, chopped
- 4 garlic cloves, crushed
- 1 400g/14oz can chopped tomatoes
- 100g/3½ oz asparagus, chopped
- 2 celery stalks, chopped

- 1 onion chopped
- ½ tsp fennel seeds
- 1 tbsp dried basil
- 1lt/4 cups fish broth/stock
- 250g/9oz raw shrimps
- Salt & Pepper to taste

Method

1 Mix together all the ingredients, except the fish, aspargus and shrimps in the crock pot.

2 Season, cover and leave to cook on low for 4-5 hours or high for 2-3 hours.

3 Meanwhile season the fish and shrimps. 45 mins before the end of cooking add the fish, shrimps and aspargus. Continue to cook until the seafood is cooked right through..

4 Try bulking this up with courgette noodles as a soup 'stew'.

CHEFS NOTE
Feel free to use any type of meaty white fish you like and, if you feel adventurous, you could add some squid, octopus or clams to the stew.

CARIBBEAN SPICED SCALLOPS

200 calories per serving

Ingredients

- 200g/7oz ripe plum tomatoes, roughly chopped
- 500g/1lb 2oz prepared fresh scallops
- 250ml/1 cup fish stock
- ½ tsp each ground all spice, chilli powder, cilantro/coriander & paprika
- 1 bunch scallions/spring onions roughly chopped
- 2 large romaine lettuces, shredded
- 2 red peppers, sliced
- 2 tsp olive oil
- Salt & pepper to taste

Method

1 First gently sauté the peppers & plum tomatoes in the olive oil oil for a few minutes until softened.

2 Place the scallops, stock, dried spices, spring onions, sautéed peppers & plum tomatoes in the crock pot.

3 Gently combine, cover and leave to cook on high for 45 minutes - 1 hour or until the scallops are cooked through.

4 Gently lift the scallops, tomatoes & peppers out of the crock pot.

5 Season and serve with the shredded lettuce.

CHEFS NOTE
Sauteed diced pumpkin makes a great side to this Caribbean dish.

FRESH MACKEREL & SUMMER SEASON PEPPERS

190 calories per serving

Ingredients

- 2 yellow or orange peppers, sliced
- 2 onions, sliced
- 1 garlic clove, crushed
- 1 red chilli, finely sliced
- 250ml/1 cup fish stock
- 400g/14oz fresh whole mackerel, gutted
- 200g/7oz ripe plum tomatoes, chopped
- 2 tbsp tomato puree
- 200g/7oz rocket
- 2 tsp olive oil
- Salt & pepper to taste

Method

1 Gently sauté the peppers, onions, garlic & chilli in a the olive oil until softened.

2 Add the sautéed vegetables to the crock pot along with all the other ingredients, except the rocket.

3 Gently combine, cover and leave to cook on low for 4-6 hours or until the fish is tender and cooked through.

4 Gently lift out of the crock pot (try to keep the fish whole), season and serve with the rocket leaves.

CHEFS NOTE
Use yellow or orange peppers rather than un-ripened green peppers.

LIME SHRIMPS WITH BABY SPINACH LEAVES

280 calories per serving

Ingredients

- 750g/1lb 11oz raw shelled jumbo shrimps/king prawns
- 250ml/1 cup coconut milk
- 2 tbsp lime juice
- 1 tbsp Thai fish sauce
- 1 red chilli, finely sliced
- 200g/7oz baby spinach leaves
- 4 tbsp freshly chopped cilantro/coriander
- 2 tsp olive oil
- Salt & pepper to taste

Method

1 Place the shrimps, coconut milk, lime juice, fish sauce, chilli & spinach in the crock pot.

2 Gently combine, cover and leave to cook on high for 45 minutes - 1 hour or until the shrimps are cooked through.

3 Serve the shrimps and coconut milk with freshly chopped coriander sprinkled on top.

CHEFS NOTE

Spinach is in season throughout late spring and summer. Baby leaves are the most sweet and tender.

VEGETABLE DISHES

CAJUN SPRING GREENS

90 calories per serving

Ingredients

- 1 tbsp Cajun seasoning (or make your own by mixing ½ tsp each paprika, cayenne pepper, sea salt, black pepper, cumin & ground garlic)
- 1 garlic clove, crushed
- 500g/1lb 2oz shredded spring greens
- 250ml/1 cup vegetable broth/stock
- Lemon wedges to serve
- Salt & pepper to taste

Method

1 Add the spring greens, stock, Cajun seasoning & garlic to the crock pot.

2 Cover and leave to cook on high for 2-4 hours or until the stock has reduced and the spring greens are tender.

3 Remove from the crock pot, drain any stock, check the seasoning and serve with lemon wedges.

CHEFS NOTE
Handy bags of prepared shredded spring greens are readily available in most grocery stores.

MOZZARELLA & BASIL TOMATOES

220 calories per serving

Ingredients

- 1 tbsp olive oil
- 2 garlic cloves, crushed
- 2 tsp balsamic vinegar
- 8 large beef tomatoes
- 3 tbsp water

- 200g/7oz mozzarella cheese, roughly chopped
- 3 tbsp freshly chopped basil
- Salt & pepper to taste

Method

1 Mix the oil, garlic & balsamic vinegar together.

2 Halve the tomatoes and brush with the sweet garlic oil.

3 Place in the crock pot, with the water, cover and leave to cook on low for 4-6 hours (add a little more water during cooking if needed).

4 When the tomatoes are tender sprinkle each on top with mozzarella cheese and continue cooking until the cheese melts.

5 Remove from the crock pot, sprinkle with basil and serve.

CHEFS NOTE
Cook the tomatoes long enough for them to be super-tender but not so that they lose their form and fall apart.

SUMMER CRUSTLESS QUICHE

200 calories per serving

Ingredients

- 200g/7oz cherry tomatoes, halved
- 1 red pepper, sliced
- 1 yellow pepper, sliced
- 125g/4oz courgettes, diced
- 125g/4oz egg plant/aubergine, diced
- 125g/4oz green beans
- 2 garlic cloves, crushed
- 1 tsp dried mixed herbs
- 1 onion, sliced
- 6 free range eggs
- 200g/7oz rocket
- 2 tsp olive oil
- Salt & pepper to taste

Method

1 Place the tomatoes, peppers, courgettes, egg plant/aubergines, green beans, garlic, herbs & sliced onions in the crock pot along with the olive oil.

2 Combine, cover and leave to cook on high for 2 hours.

3 Break the eggs into a bowl, gently whisk and pour into the crock pot.

4 Quickly combine for a few seconds. Replace the lid and leave to cook for a further 1-1½ hours or until the eggs are set and the vegetables are tender.

5 Gently lift out of the crock pot.

6 Slice into thick wedges and serve with the rocket leaves.

CHEFS NOTE

This type of crust-less quiche is popular in Italy. Use whichever keto vegetables you have to hand to create your own version.

PORTABELLA MUSHROOMS & DOLCELATTE CHEESE

220 calories per serving

Ingredients

- 600g/1lb 5oz portabella mushrooms, thickly sliced
- 2 garlic cloves, crushed
- 60ml/¼ cup vegetable broth/stock
- 1 tbsp lemon juice
- 150g/5oz dolcelatte/gorgonzola cheese
- 2 tbsp freshly chopped basil
- 2 tsp olive oil
- Salt & pepper to taste

Method

1 Place the mushrooms, garlic, stock & lemon juice in the crock pot.

2 Combine, cover and leave to cook on high for 2-4 hours or until most of the liquid has disappeared.

3 Stir in the dolcelatte/gorgonzola cheese and fresh basil.

4 Check the seasoning and serve.

CHEFS NOTE
These delicious mushrooms can be served as a luxurious side dish.

POMODORO PASTA SAUCE

Ingredients

- 2 400g/14oz cans chopped tomatoes
- 6 large fresh tomatoes (vine ripened are best)
- 250ml/1 cup tomato sauce/passata
- Bunch fresh basil chopped (reserve a little some for garnish)
- 3 garlic cloves, crushed
- 1 onion, chopped
- 1 tsp extra virgin olive oil
- Salt and pepper to taste
- Handful sliced black olives

Method

1 Combine all the ingredients in the crock pot and cover.

2 Leave to cook on low for 5-6 hours or high for 3-4 hours. Delicious served with keto friendly pasta, salad & grated parmesan cheese.

CHEFS NOTE

This is a simple tomato based Italian sauce which gets better the longer you leave it. Reheated leftovers often have a greater depth of taste which is worth waiting for.

VEGGIE TURMERIC SOY BEANS

234 calories per serving

Ingredients

- 2 400g/14oz cans black sot beans, drained
- 2 onions, chopped
- 1 tbsp tomato puree/paste
- 2 cloves garlic, crushed
- 1 tsp fresh grated ginger or ½ teaspoon ground ginger
- 2 tsp garam masala
- 1 tsp each ground cumin & cilantro/coriander
- 2 tsp turmeric
- ½ tsp chilli powder
- 200g/7oz fresh spinach
- 3 tbsp lemon juice
- 250ml/1 cup veg broth/stock
- Salt & pepper to taste

Method

1 Combine all the ingredients, except the lemon juice and spinach, in the crock pot.

2 Cook on low for 5-6 hours or on high for 3-4 hours with the lid tightly shut. Add a little more stock during cooking if needed.

3 Ensure the beans are cooked though, stir in the lemon juice and spinach to serve.

CHEFS NOTE

Black soy beans are a useful low carb keto ingredient which differ from the high carb content of most other beans.

TOMATO & GARLIC MUSHROOMS

180 calories per serving

Ingredients

- 1 tbsp olive oil
- 450g/1lb chestnut mushrooms
- 5 cloves garlic, crushed
- 1 stick celery
- 400g/14oz can chopped tomatoes
- 1 tbsp tomato puree/paste
- 3 tbsp fresh chopped flat leaf parsley
- ½ tsp crushed chilli flakes
- 1 onion, chopped

Method

1 Add all the ingredients to the crock pot, except the parsley.

2 Season, cover and leave to cook on high for 3-4 hours or low for 5-6 hours or until the mushrooms are tender and the flavours have thoroughly blended.

CHEFS NOTE
This is great served with cougette spaghetti or cauliflower 'rice'.

FENNEL 'RISOTTO'

335 calories per serving

Ingredients

- 1 fennel bulb, diced
- 250g/9oz cauliflower 'rice'
- 2 tbsp grated parmesan cheese
- 125g/4oz black olives, finely chopped
- 3 garlic cloves, crushed

- 1lt/4 cups vegetable broth/stock
- 50g/2oz rocket
- 1 tbsp butter butter
- Salt & pepper to taste

Method

1 Preheat the crock pot and place the butter in the bottom. When it is melted add all the ingredients, except the cheese and rocket, to the crock pot and season well.

2 Cover and leave to cook on high for 2-3 hours. If you need to add more liquid during cooking go ahead by adding just a little each time.

3 After cooking, all the liquid should be absorbed. If it isn't, leave to cook for a little longer with the lid off.

4 Serve sprinkled with parmesan cheese and the rocket piled on top.

CHEFS NOTE
Risotto usually needs a lot of stirring during cooking but not with this cauliflower 'rice' based dish.required.

WILD MUSHROOM STROGANOFF

Ingredients

- 600g/1lb 5oz wild mixed mushrooms sliced
- 2 onions, chopped
- 4 garlic cloves, crushed
- 2 tsp smoked paprika
- 250ml/1 cup vegetable broth/stock
- 400g/14oz can condensed mushroom soup
- Bunch flat chopped leaf parsley (reserve a little for garnish)

Method

1 Add all the ingredients into the crock pot. Close the lid tightly and leave to cook on high for 2-3 hours or low for 4-5 hours.

2 Ensure the mushrooms are tender and serve with a spoon of Greek yogurt.

CHEFS NOTE

The more exciting the mushrooms the better this dish is going to taste. Use whatever you can get your hands on but a combination of portobello, shitake, morel, oyster and enoki would be fantastic. However don't be put off if you can only get regular varieties - it will still taste good!

SPICED SWEET POTATOES

Ingredients

- 500g/1lb 2oz cubed sweet potatoes
- 1 onion, chopped
- 1 garlic clove, crushed
- 1 tsp each ground cilantro/coriander, turmeric & cumin
- ½ each tsp ground ginger, paprika & mustard seeds

- 120ml/ ½ cup vegetable broth/stock
- 2 tbsp freshly chopped cilantro/coriander
- 2 tbsp butter butter
- Salt & pepper to taste

Method

1 Add all the ingredients, except coriander to the crock pot, cover and leave to cook on high for 2-3 hours .

2 Add a little more stock or water during cooking if needed. If there is too much liquid, take the lid off and leave to cook on high for approx 40 mins.

3 Sprinkle the chopped coriander over the top and serve.

CHEFS NOTE
Sweet potato is acceptable as an 'occasional' ingredient on the keto diet, or try this recipe with pumpkin which is even more keto friendly.

BLACK SOY BEAN & ALMOND STEW

288 calories per serving

Ingredients

- 1 onion, sliced into rounds
- 2 garlic cloves, crushed
- 300g/11oz pumpkin, diced
- 1 tsp mustard seeds
- 2 tbsp tomato puree/paste
- ½ tsp ground cinnamon
- 1 celery stick, chopped

- 450g/1lb cauliflower florets
- 200g/7oz canned black soy beans, drained
- 75g/3oz chopped almonds
- 400g/14oz canned chopped tomatoes
- 250ml/1 cup vegetable broth/stock
- Salt & pepper to taste

Method

1 Add all the ingredients to the crock pot.

2 Cover, stir well and leave to cook on high for 2-3 hours or low for 4-5 hours or until the vegetables are tender.

CHEFS NOTE

If you want the stew a little thicker, take the lid off and continue to cook on high for 45mins or until the consistency is to your liking.

SOUPS

....

HOCK HAM & LEEK SOUP

158 calories per serving

Ingredients

- 2 ham knuckles (get them smoked if you can)
- 2 celery stalks, chopped
- 2 leeks, chopped
- 2 onions, chopped
- 3 garlic cloves, crushed
- 1 ½ lt/6 cups chicken broth/stock

Method

1 Combine all the ingredients into the crock pot and cook on low for 5-6 hours or high for 3-4 hours with the lid tightly shut.

2 When the soup is cooked, take out the hocks and strip the meat - if they are fully cooked the meat should fall away easily.

3 Discard any fat and stir the shredded ham back into the soup.

CHEFS NOTE

Ham hocks are a bargain ingredient that can give a real depth to a dish. You could substitute ham hocks for a meaty ham bone if you had one left after a family gathering.

SQUASH, BASIL & TOMATO SOUP

130 calories per serving

Ingredients

- 400g/14oz butternut squash flesh, cubed
- 8 fresh vine tomatoes, chopped
- 2 tbsp freshly chopped basil leaves
- 4 tbsp tomato puree/paste

- 1lt/4 cups vegetable broth/stock
- 60ml/¼ cup single cream
- Salt & pepper to taste

Method

1 Place all the ingredients, except the cream, in the crock pot. Season, cover and leave to cook on low for 3-4 hours or until the vegetables are tender.

2 After cooking blend the soup to a smooth consistency and serve with a swirl of fresh cream.

CHEFS NOTE

Butternut squash is a perfect crock pot ingredient. Its creamy, firm texture holds well during cooking and forms a robust base to this tasty soup.

SPANISH SAUSAGE SOUP

140 calories per serving

Ingredients

- 450g/1lb cauliflower florets, finely chopped
- 1 tbsp olive oil
- 750ml/3 cups vegetable broth/stock
- 250ml/1 cup semi milk

- 2 tbsp freshly chopped flat leaf parsley
- 1 tsp smoked paprika
- 100g/3½ oz chorizo sausage, finely chopped
- Salt & pepper to taste

Method

1 Place all the ingredients, except the parsley, in the crock pot.

2 Season, cover and leave to cook on low for 3-4 hours or until the vegetables are tender.

3 Adjust the seasoning and serve with the parsley sprinkled on top.

CHEFS NOTE

if you wanted a smoother version of the soup remove 2 ladels of soup. Blend the remaining soup and return the 2 ladels to the pot.

ST.PATRICK'S DAY SOUP

130 calories per serving

Ingredients

- 300g/11oz sweet potatoes chopped
- 1 onion, chopped
- 3 leeks, chopped
- Salt & pepper to taste
- 500ml/2 cups milk
- 750ml/3 cups vegetable broth/stock

Method

1 Combine all the ingredients together in the crock pot and leave to cook on low for 4-5 hours with the lid tightly shut.

2 Make sure the potatoes are tender, season to taste and then either blend as a smooth soup or eat it rough, ready and rustic with some crusty keto friendly bread.

3 You can also add a garnish of chopped chives and sour cream or crème fraiche if you want to add an extra touch.

CHEFS NOTE
Sweet potato is acceptable as an 'occasional' ingredient on the keto diet, or try this recipe with pumpkin which is even more keto friendly.

SPICY CABBAGE SOUP

211 calories per serving

Ingredients

- 2 tsp ground cumin
- ½ tsp crushed chilli flakes
- 1 tbsp olive oil
- 750g/1lb 11oz cabbage finely chopped
- ½ onion, finely chopped
- 750ml/3 cups vegetable broth/stock
- 120ml/½ cup milk
- 60ml/¼ cup single cream
- Salt & pepper to taste.

Method

1 Add all the ingredients to the crock pot, except the cream and milk. Season, cover and leave to cook on high for approx 3 hours.

2 Add the milk and warm through for a minute or two. Use a food processor or blender to whizz the soup to a smooth consistency and serve with a swirl of single cream in each bowl.

CHEFS NOTE
This warming soup can be tweaked to suit your taste - add more or less chilli flakes as you prefer.

SOY & SAVOY SOUP

220 calories per serving

Ingredients

- 1 onion, finely chopped
- 1 whole savoy cabbage, chopped
- 1 tbsp olive oil
- 1lt/4 cups vegetable broth/stock
- 2 tbsp tomato puree/paste
- 1 tsp each dried oregano & rosemary
- Salt & Pepper to taste
- 400g/14oz canned black soy beans, drained

Method

1 Place all the ingredients in the crock pot. Season, cover and leave to cook on low for 3-4 hours or until the vegetables are tender.

2 Adjust the seasoning and serve.

CHEFS NOTE
Black soy beans are a useful low carb keto ingredient which differ from the high carb content of most other beans.

PUMPKIN & COCONUT MILK SOUP

238 calories per serving

Ingredients

- 1 onion, chopped
- 500g/1lb 2oz pumpkin flesh, diced
- 1 tsp each turmeric, cumin, cilantro/ coriander & paprika
- 120ml/½ cup coconut milk
- 2 tbsp freshly chopped chives
- 750ml/3 cups vegetable broth/stock
- Salt & pepper to taste
- 250ml/1 cup Greek yogurt

Method

1 Place all the ingredients, except the chives, coconut milk & yogurt in the crock pot. Season, cover and leave to cook on low for 3-4 hours or until the vegetables are tender.

2 After cooking, blend the soup to a smooth consistency. Stir through the coconut milk and serve with a dollop of yogurt in the middle and some fresh chives sprinkled on top.

CHEFS NOTE

Adding the coconut milk during lengthy cooking risks the milk 'splitting', so leave it until the end to warm through.

SPINACH SOUP

190 calories per serving

Ingredients

- 2 lt/8 cups vegetable broth/stock
- 4 tbsp tomato puree/paste
- 250g/9oz caulifower 'rice'
- 200g/7oz spinach, finely chopped

- 2 onions, chopped
- 2 garlic cloves, crushed
- 1 tsp each dried basil & oregano
- Salt & pepper to taste

Method

1 Combine all the ingredients, except the spinach, into the crock pot.

2 Season, cover and leave to cook on low for 5-6 hours or high for 3-4 hours. 20 minutes before the end of cooking, stir through the spinach and serve (blend if you prefer a smooth consistency)

CHEFS NOTE

This hearty soup is great freshened up with a twist of lemon and chopped basil to garnish.

SUMMER SALADS

....

GREEK EGG PLANT SALAD

230
calories per
serving

Ingredients

- 3 egg plant/aubergines, cut into 3cm cubes
- 1 onion, sliced
- ½ tsp each ground nutmeg & cinnamon
- 1 garlic clove, crushed
- 1 tbsp lemon juice
- 2 tbsp extra virgin olive oil
- 200g/7oz mixed leaves
- 2 keto flat breads, cut into 3cm fingers
- 4 tbsp Greek yogurt
- Lemon wedges to serve
- Salt & pepper to taste

Method

1 Combine the egg plant/aubergines, onions, dried spices, garlic, lemon juice & olive oil in the crock pot. Cover and leave to cook on high for 2-3 hours or until the aubergine cubes are tender and still have their shape.

2 Season and arrange on plates in the centre of the mixed leaves.

3 Share the pitta bread fingers between the plates and add a dollop of Greek yogurt to the side.

4 Serve with the lemon wedges.

CHEFS NOTE
You could sprinkle a little paprika over the Greek yogurt if you have it.

SPANISH CHORIZO SALAD

190 calories per serving

Ingredients

- 150g/5oz chorizo sausage, diced
- 1 onion, sliced
- 1 red pepper, sliced
- 2 garlic cloves, crushed
- 400g/14oz vine ripened tomatoes, quartered
- 1 tbsp water
- Pinch of salt
- 200g/7oz mixed leaves
- 3 tbsp freshly chopped flat leaf parsley
- Salt & pepper to taste

Method

1 Combine the diced chorizo, onion, peppers, garlic, tomatoes & salt in the crock pot.

2 Cover and leave to cook on high for 2-3 hours or until tender and cooked through.

3 Season and arrange on plates with the mixed salad leaves.

CHEFS NOTE

This dish is also great served on top of keto friendly crispbreads or rice cakes.

BEEF & CHILLI SALAD

300 calories per serving

Ingredients

- 400g/14oz lean braising steak, cut into strips
- 2 red chillies, sliced
- 2 tsp freshly grated ginger
- 1 onion, sliced
- 1 red pepper, sliced
- 2 garlic cloves, finely sliced
- 250ml/1 cup beef broth/stock
- 200g/7oz baby leaf salad
- 2 tbsp freshly chopped flat leaf parsley
- Salt & pepper to taste

Method

1 Combine the steak, chillies, ginger, onions, peppers, garlic & stock in the crock pot.

2 Cover and leave to cook on low for 6-8 hours or until the beef is super tender (add a little more stock during cooking if needed).

3 Season and arrange on plates with the baby leaf salad and chopped parsley.

CHEFS NOTE

You could garnish with freshly chopped coriander to add a different twist to the salad.

ANCHOVY & BROCCOLI SALAD

165 calories per serving

Ingredients

- 400g/14oz tenderstem broccoli, roughly chopped
- 200g/7oz black soy beans, sliced
- 6 canned anchovy fillets, drained
- ½ tsp crushed chilli flakes
- 1 onion, sliced
- 2 garlic cloves, crushed
- 120ml/½ cup vegetable broth/stock
- 4 baby gem lettuces, shredded
- Lemon wedges to serve
- Salt & pepper to taste

Method

1 Combine all the ingredients, except the lettuce & lemon wedges, in the crock pot.

2 Cover and leave to cook on high for 2-4 hours or until everything is tender tender.

3 Season and arrange on plates with the lettuce and lemon wedges.

CHEFS NOTE
You could also toss this dish through 'miracle' no carb noodles to make a more substantial meal (leave out the lettuce).

SIMPLE SHREDDED CHICKEN SALAD

220
calories per
serving

Ingredients

- 500g/1lb 2oz skinless chicken breasts
- 1 garlic clove, crushed
- 500ml/2 cups chicken broth/stock
- ½ tsp paprika
- 1 tsp mixed dried herbs

- 200g/7oz cherry tomatoes, halved
- 2 large romaine lettuces, shredded
- 2 tbsp freshly chopped flat leaf parsley
- Salt & pepper to taste

Method

1 Combine the chicken, garlic, stock, paprika & dried herbs in the crock pot. Cover and leave to cook on high for 3-4 hours or until the chicken is super tender.

2 Remove the chicken breasts and use two forks to shred.

3 Serve with the fresh cherry tomatoes, shredded lettuce & chopped parsley.

4 Drizzle some of the stock juices over the top of the salad if you wish.

CHEFS NOTE
This is a wonderful summertime staple that can be served hot or cold

PESTO & TOMATO CHICKEN SALAD

240 calories per serving

Ingredients

- 500g/1lb 2oz skinless chicken breasts
- 200g/7oz cherry tomatoes, halved
- 2 tbsp green pesto
- 200g/7oz mixed baby leaf salad
- 2 tbsp freshly chopped flat leaf parsley
- Salt & pepper to taste

Method

1 Combine the chicken, tomatoes, & pesto in the crock pot. Cover and leave to cook on high for 3-4 hours or until the chicken is super tender (add a little water during cooking if needed).

2 Remove the chicken breasts and use two forks to shred.

3 Arrange the shredded chicken with the cooked cherry tomatoes on top of the mixed leaves.

4 Sprinkle with chopped parsley & serve.

CHEFS NOTE
Shop-bought pesto is fine, or try making your own if you have a plentiful supply of fresh basil.

TURKEY 'TACO' SALAD

210 calories per serving

Ingredients

- 350g/12oz lean turkey mince
- 200g/7oz ripe tomatoes, chopped
- 1 tbsp tomato puree/paste
- 1 onion, finely chopped
- 200g/7oz black soy beans
- 1 red pepper, chopped

- 2 tbsp taco seasoning
- 60ml/¼ cup chicken broth/stock
- 4 baby gem lettuces, shredded
- 2 tbsp Greek yogurt
- 1 tbsp freshly chopped flat leaf parsley
- Salt & pepper to taste

Method

1 Combine the mince, tomatoes, puree, onions, sweetcorn, peppers, taco seasoning & stock in the crock pot.

2 Cover and leave to cook on high for 2-3 hours or low for 4-5 hours or until the mince is tender and cooked through.

3 Arrange on top of the lettuce with a dollop of yogurt, sprinkled with chopped parsley.

CHEFS NOTE
Use canned chopped tomatoes if you don't have any fresh to hand.

CONVERSION CHART: DRY INGREDIENTS

Metric	Imperial
7g	¼ oz
15g	½ oz
20g	¾ oz
25g	1 oz
40g	1½oz
50g	2oz
60g	2½oz
75g	3oz
100g	3½oz
125g	4oz
140g	4½oz
150g	5oz
165g	5½oz
175g	6oz
200g	7oz
225g	8oz
250g	9oz
275g	10oz
300g	11oz
350g	12oz
375g	13oz
400g	14oz

Metric	Imperial
425g	15oz
450g	1lb
500g	1lb 2oz
550g	1¼lb
600g	1lb 5oz
650g	1lb 7oz
675g	1½lb
700g	1lb 9oz
750g	1lb 11oz
800g	1¾lb
900g	2lb
1kg	2¼lb
1.1kg	2½lb
1.25kg	2¾lb
1.35kg	3lb
1.5kg	3lb 6oz
1.8kg	4lb
2kg	4½lb
2.25kg	5lb
2.5kg	5½lb
2.75kg	6lb

CONVERSION CHART: LIQUID MEASURES

Metric	Imperial	US
25ml	1fl oz	
60ml	2fl oz	¼ cup
75ml	2½ fl oz	
100ml	3½fl oz	
120ml	4fl oz	½ cup
150ml	5fl oz	
175ml	6fl oz	
200ml	7fl oz	
250ml	8½ fl oz	1 cup
300ml	10½ fl oz	
360ml	12½ fl oz	
400ml	14fl oz	
450ml	15½ fl oz	
600ml	1 pint	
750ml	1¼ pint	3 cups
1 litre	1½ pints	4 cups